HOW YOUR BODY WORKS

SENSING THE WORLD

THE NERVOUS SYSTEM

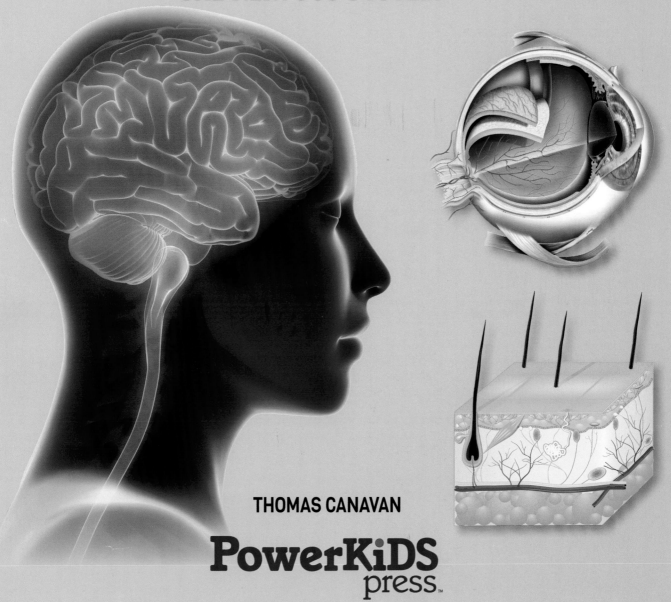

THOMAS CANAVAN

PowerKiDS
press™

Published in 2016 by
The Rosen Publishing Group, Inc.
29 East 21st Street, New York, NY 10010

Cataloging-in-Publication Data
Canavan, Thomas.
Sensing the world: the nervous system / by Thomas Canavan.
p. cm. — (How your body works)
Includes index.
ISBN 978-1-4994-1232-1 (pbk.)
ISBN 978-1-4994-1254-3 (6 pack)
ISBN 978-1-4994-1248-2 (library binding)
1. Nervous system — Juvenile literature. I. Canavan, Thomas, 1956-. II. Title.
QP361.5 C218 2016
612.8—d23

Produced by Arcturus Publishing Limited,

Author: Thomas Canavan
Editors: Joe Harris, Joe Fullman, Nicola Barber and Sam Williams
Designer: Elaine Wilkinson
Original design concept and cover design: Notion Design

Picture Credits: Key: b-bottom, m-middle, l-left, r-right, t-top. All images
courtesy of Shutterstock, apart from: Corbis: p18 b. Lee Montgomery and Anne
Sharp: back cover, p30, p31. Science Photo Library: p2 tl, p3 tr, p3 m, p14 tl,
p15 tl (Steve Gschmeissner), p17 ml (Jacobin/BSIP), p11 (Omikron).

Manufactured in the United States of America
CPSIA Compliance Information: Batch #WS15PK:
For Further Information contact Rosen Publishing, New York, New York at 1-800-237-9932

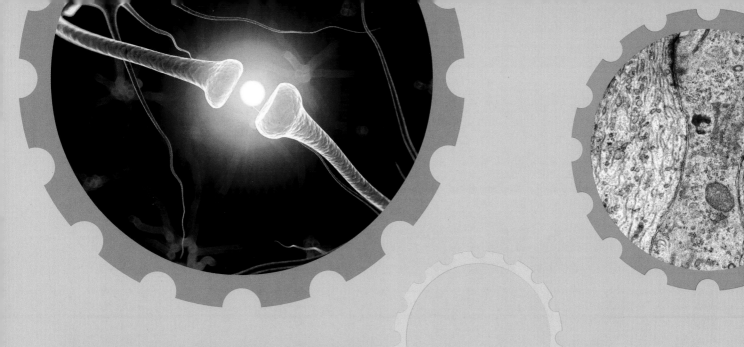

CONTENTS

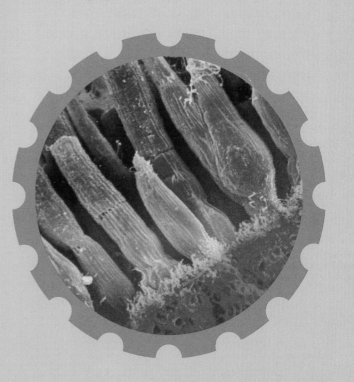

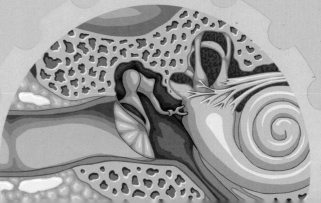

TAKING
CONTROL

Just like the conductor of an orchestra, your brain is making decisions and guiding you all the time. Different areas of your brain concentrate on special jobs. Some of those jobs need quick action – like telling your body which muscles to use when you're running or swimming. Others, like doing your homework, take more time.

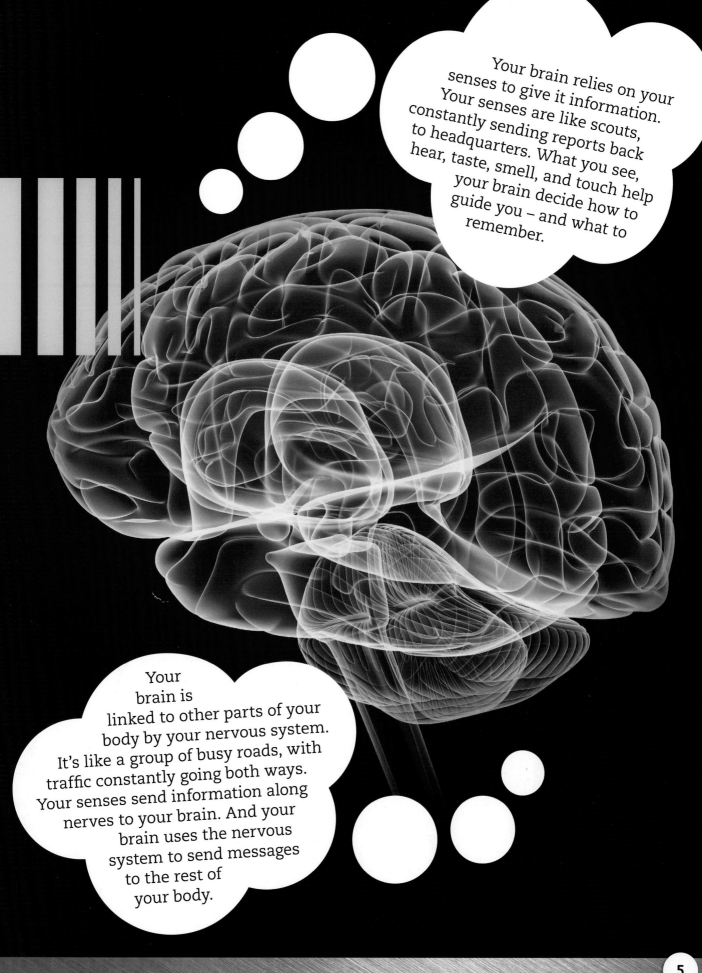

Your brain relies on your senses to give it information. Your senses are like scouts, constantly sending reports back to headquarters. What you see, hear, taste, smell, and touch help your brain decide how to guide you – and what to remember.

Your brain is linked to other parts of your body by your nervous system. It's like a group of busy roads, with traffic constantly going both ways. Your senses send information along nerves to your brain. And your brain uses the nervous system to send messages to the rest of your body.

Brain stem

Cerebrum

THE BRAIN IS BOSS

Your brain is the boss of your body. It is constantly checking new information, storing the things you learn and the experiences you have, and sending orders out to your body, telling it what to do.

YOUR HARD DRIVE

Your brain weighs around 3 pounds (1.5 kg) and looks a lot like a wrinkled grapefruit. Inside it are about 100 billion nerve cells, the headquarters of your nervous system. The human brain is often compared to a computer. It sends and receives signals to the rest of your body through the spinal cord, which extends down from it. Each part of your brain is responsible for a special job. It could be deciding whether you feel angry, which muscles to use or whether to put on a warmer coat.

SORRY – WRONG DEPARTMENT

Different parts of your brain concentrate on different jobs. The largest part is the cerebrum, which is the part you'd see if you took the top of your head off. This is where your thinking gets done and where you store your memories. The cerebellum, at the back of your brain, controls all your movements. Your brain stem connects your brain with your spinal cord, and it looks after activities such as digestion, blood flow, and breathing.

Spinal cord

Cerebellum

AUTO PILOT

At first, some things such as riding a bike or learning a dance routine, need concentration and practice. But after a while, your cerebellum takes over and remembers how to do these things, so you can do them automatically "without thinking."

ACTIVITY

Put a dozen different objects on a tray. Ask your friends to look at the objects for one minute. Then, remove the tray. Now, ask your friends to write down as many of the objects as they are able to remember. Which one of your friends is the best at this kind of mental task?

LEFT OR RIGHT?

Your cerebrum has two halves – left and right. The left half seems to be linked to "practical" actions such as mathematics and speech. The right half concentrates on more "artistic" things such as music and recognizing faces. You use both halves, but right-handed people seem to use their left half more, and left-handers seem to use their right half more!

Your brain operates on the same amount of power used by a 10-watt light bulb!

WHAT A NERVE!

Brain

Your brain and spinal cord are linked to a huge network of nerves. These carry information all around your body. Together, they make up your nervous system. In just a fraction of a second, messages are sent back and forth from your brain, deciding all that you do and think.

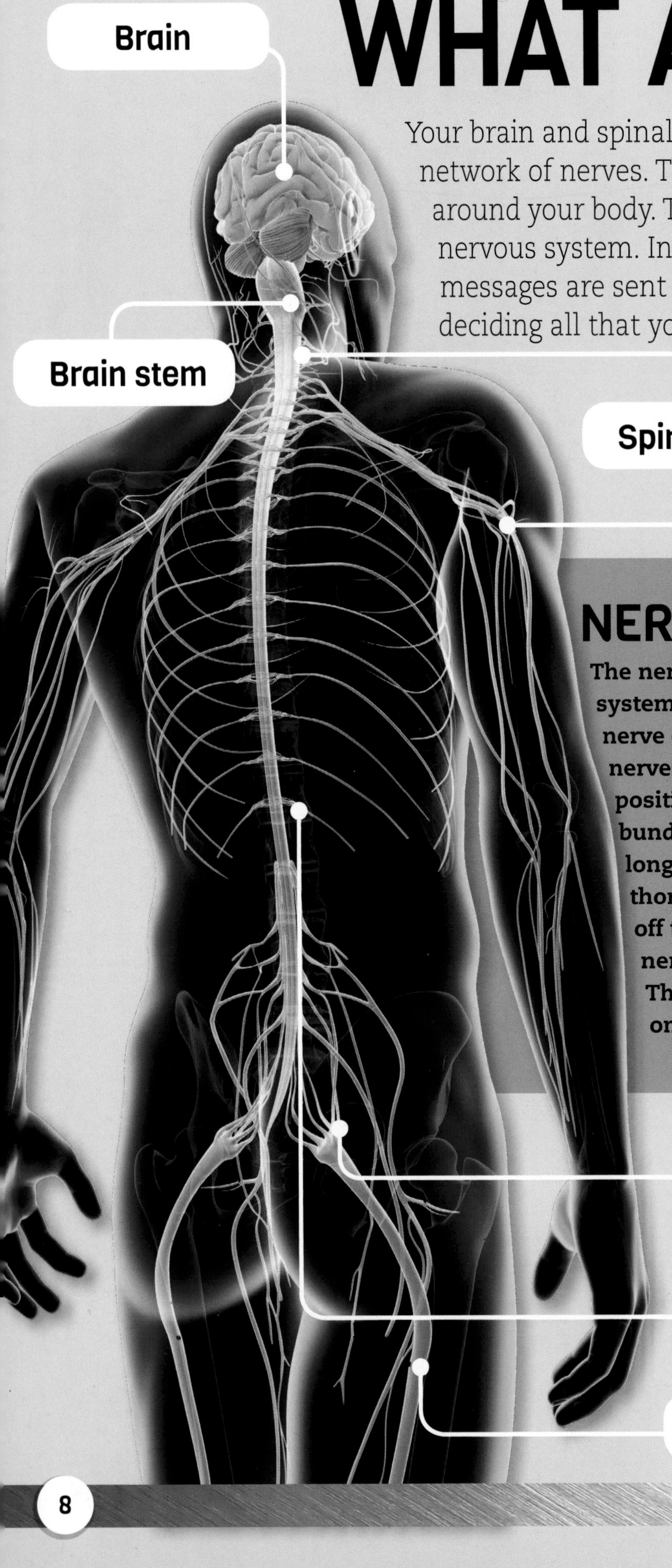

Brain stem

Spinal cord

Radial nerve

NERVE NETWORK

The nerves that make up the nervous system are actually narrow threads of nerve cells, or neurons. Many of the major nerves are named after their job, or their position in the body. The spinal cord is a long bundle of nerves, about 15 inches (40 cm) long, with 31 pairs of nerves (including the thoracic and lumbar nerves). These branch off to the rest of your body. The sciatic nerve is the largest nerve in the body. The radial nerve starts at the radius, one of the the bones in your arm.

Lumbar nerves

Thoracic nerves

Sciatic nerve

TO AND FRO

Nerves take information to and from the brain. Sensory neurons send messages from the body to the brain. Motor neurons carry messages from the brain to the muscles to tell them when and how to move. Other neurons send information between the sensory and motor neurons.

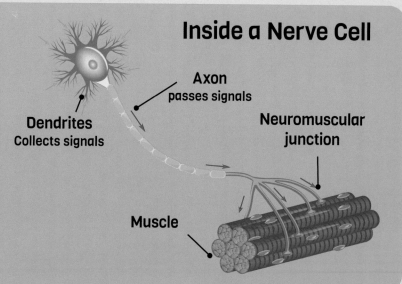

Axon
passes signals

Neuromuscular junction

Dendrites
Collects signals

Muscle

HOW SHOCKING

Neurons pick up and send signals as electrical pulses. The electric signal creates a chemical change at the synapse – the place where two neurons join together. This allows the electrical pulse to jump across the gap. The pulse continues along like this, neuron by neuron, as it passes all along the nerve – and this all happens in less than a second!

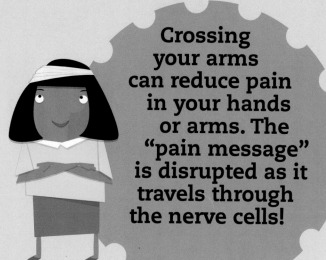

Crossing your arms can reduce pain in your hands or arms. The "pain message" is disrupted as it travels through the nerve cells!

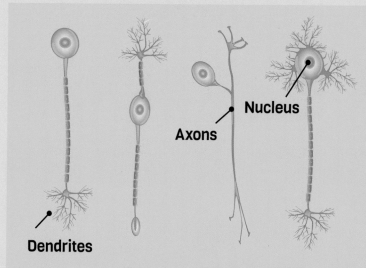

Nucleus

Axons

Dendrites

CHAIN REACTION

Neurons come in many different shapes, but they all have a nucleus and special parts called dendrites and axons. Dendrites picks up signals from other neurons and axons pass them on. Neurons are lined up in long chains, but they don't actually touch. Messages travel from neuron to neuron as the signals jump across small gaps, or synapses, between them.

EYE SPY

Think of how much information you get from your eyes – playing games, watching films or reading this page. Your eyes constantly receive images, focus them, and then send signals to your brain. They tell you what's around you, how close or big things are, whether they're moving and much more.

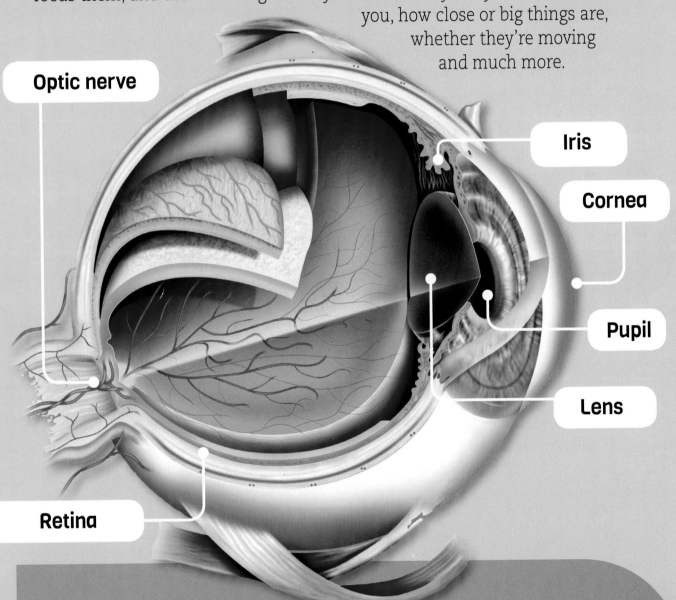

Optic nerve

Iris

Cornea

Pupil

Lens

Retina

IT'S CLEAR TO SEE

Whenever you look at an object, the light from it enters your eye through your pupil, the dark opening in the middle of your eye. The iris then changes the size of the pupil, depending on how bright the light is. The lens focuses the light onto the retina at the back of your eye. Here, the light is turned into an electrical burst which travels along the optic nerve to the brain, where an image of what you are seeing is formed.

TWO EYES ARE BETTER THAN ONE

Why do you have two eyes? It's to help you judge how far away things are. When you look at something, your two eyes see the image slightly differently. The difference depends on how far away an object is. Your brain receives both images and instantly works out the distance to the object. This ability is called depth perception.

3D WORLD TURNED UPSIDE DOWN

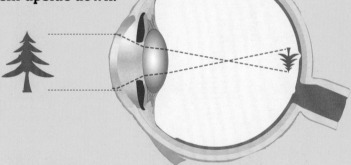

Your retina contains millions of special receptor cells, as shown on the left. They respond to light entering your eye. By focusing images on your retina, your lens turns them upside down. So, in order for you to see properly, your brain has to turn them the right way up again. Your brain also needs to merge the two slightly different images captured by each of your eyes into one. By doing so, your brain creates a 3D picture of the thing you are looking at.

ACTIVITY

Hold a pencil in each hand and straighten your arms in front of you. Close one eye and try to touch the tip of one pencil to the other. Now try it with both your eyes open. It should be a lot easier, thanks to your depth perception.

The size of your eyes barely changes from the day you're born to when you become an adult.

HEAR, HEAR!

What you hear as sounds starts out as waves in the air. Your ears pick up those sound waves and change them into signals that are sent to your brain. Your brain makes sense of the patterns in the sounds you hear, so you recognize them as music, speech, or familiar voices. Other sounds, like screams or sirens, warn you of danger.

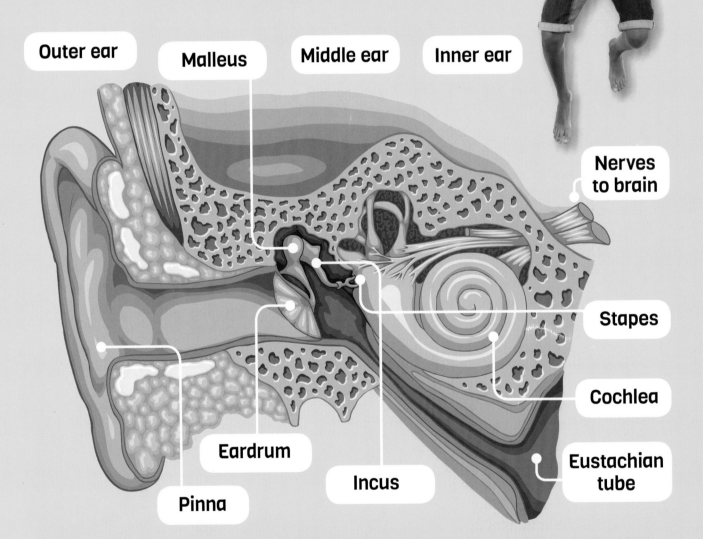

Outer ear

Malleus

Middle ear

Inner ear

Nerves to brain

Stapes

Cochlea

Eardrum

Eustachian tube

Incus

Pinna

SOUND WAVES

The pinna is the part of your outer ear that you can see. Its job is to capture sounds so that they travel down the ear canal into your middle ear. Those sound waves are turned into movements, or vibrations, in your middle ear, which are passed to your inner ear.

THE DRUM SECTION

Your eardrum is where your outer ear meets your middle ear. Sound waves make it move, or vibrate. The vibrations cause three tiny bones – the malleus, incus, and stapes – to vibrate. And those vibrations create waves in liquid inside the cochlea of the inner ear. Tiny hairs on the cochlea then pick up that movement and send signals to the nerve cells. That's where the nervous system takes over and sends the signals to the brain. And that's how you "hear" sounds.

Ears make earwax to clean and protect the ear. Tiny hairs, called cilia, move the wax forwards out of the ear!

FEELING THE PRESSURE

You sometimes get a popping feeling in your ears traveling on a mountain road or on a plane. This is because the air inside your ears is at a different pressure from the air outside your ears. As air pressure increases on the outside, it pushes in on the eardrum. To balance this out, your body takes in air through the Eustachian tubes, which connect your ears to your throat. Your ears then "pop" as the air is balanced, or equalized, on both sides of the eardrum.

WHAT'S THE FREQUENCY?

Sounds and hearing are all about vibrations. How fast or slow the sound waves are moving decides whether you hear them as high or low sounds. That speed is called the frequency – because it describes how frequently the air is vibrating. Some frequencies are too high or low for humans to hear. If you blow a dog whistle, your pet will hear it even though you can't. You lose your ability to hear some very high or very low frequencies as you get older. In fact, some phones have ring tones that grown-ups can't hear!

SMELLS GOOD, TASTES GREAT

TASTY!

The picture above shows the bumps on your tongue in close-up, called taste buds. Taste buds have special cells that pick up particular chemicals (tastes) in the food you eat. Sweet taste cells respond when you're eating chocolate or cake. Salty cells pick up signals when you're eating chips or french fries.

For a long time, scientists thought we could pick out four main tastes – sweet, sour, salty, and bitter. They now accept there's a fifth taste, called umami, which comes out strongly in meat. And they suggest that maybe you can detect six or even more tastes. You might be able to taste the calcium in vegetables, or the carbon dioxide in a can of cola.

Stick out your tongue and look at it in a mirror. You'll see lots of pink bumps. That's where your body tastes food. Special cells pick out certain tastes and send messages to your brain. Most of those cells are on your tongue, but you also have some taste cells on the roof of your mouth and the back of your throat. Meanwhile your nose helps you get a fuller picture of what you're tasting.

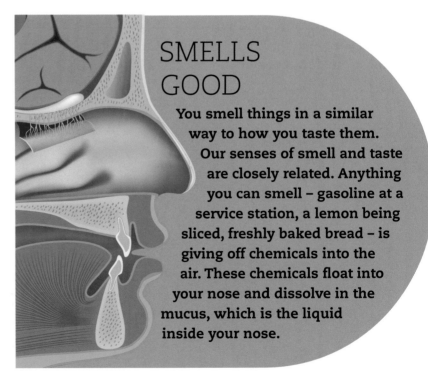

SMELLS GOOD

You smell things in a similar way to how you taste them. Our senses of smell and taste are closely related. Anything you can smell – gasoline at a service station, a lemon being sliced, freshly baked bread – is giving off chemicals into the air. These chemicals float into your nose and dissolve in the mucus, which is the liquid inside your nose.

SMELL SIGNALS

Special cells called chemoreceptors (shown here on the left) are found deep inside your nose. These react to particular dissolved chemicals. They send a signal further into your nose, and that signal then travels along nerves to different parts of your brain. Smell is an important sense. For example, if we smell smoke or gas, it can alert us to danger.

Your nose also helps you to taste things. As you chew, your food gives off chemicals. Some of them float up into your nose, which "smells" them as normal. You need this smell as much as you do the taste signals from your mouth in order to get the full picture of how your food tastes.

Tastes and smells can trigger memories that stay with you for life.

Our bodies produce certain chemicals when we're afraid, so other people might be able to "smell fear."

Your nose plays an important part in tasting. That's why you can't taste food with a bad cold!

HOW TOUCHING

Your sense of touch is important. Without it, you wouldn't know that the stove top was dangerously hot, or that the thorns on a plant were sharp enough to cut you – or even how pleasant the spring sunshine feels on your bare arm.

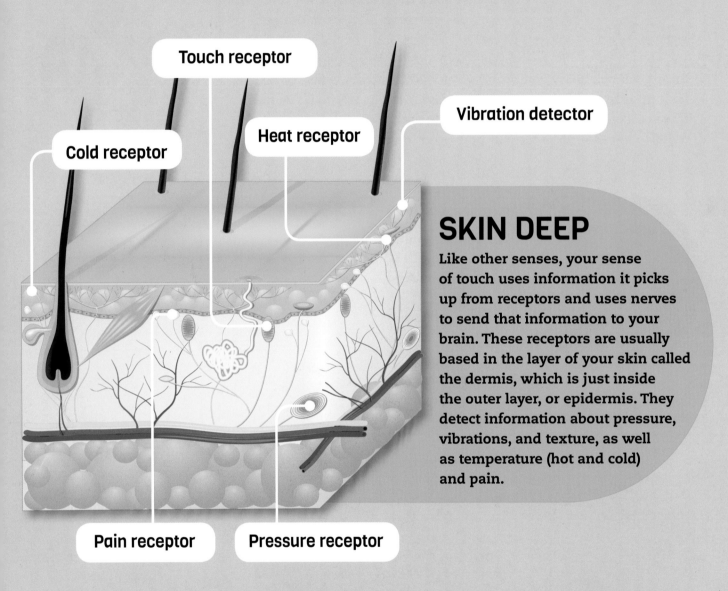

Touch receptor

Cold receptor

Heat receptor

Vibration detector

Pain receptor

Pressure receptor

SKIN DEEP

Like other senses, your sense of touch uses information it picks up from receptors and uses nerves to send that information to your brain. These receptors are usually based in the layer of your skin called the dermis, which is just inside the outer layer, or epidermis. They detect information about pressure, vibrations, and texture, as well as temperature (hot and cold) and pain.

TAKE THE HEAT OFF

Signals about heat go to and from the brain in a flash. You could be badly burned if you didn't react quickly to heat. It takes only about 15 milliseconds (thousandths of a second) for the information to reach your brain, and a similar time on the way back. That's usually enough time to get you to pull your hand away from a hot stove or kettle.

TOO COLD!

Cold receptors in your fingertips pick up information when you touch an ice cube. That sensation of cold then becomes an electrical signal that's sent along the nerves to your spinal cord, and travels directly to your brain. Your brain quickly responds to this information and sends instructions back to the motor neurons that control the muscles in your fingertips: "too cold – stop touching it."

Scientists say that our sense of touch develops "from head to toe." That's why a young baby puts new things in its mouth.

SENSITIVE BODY PARTS

This strange man (on the right) is actually a sensory body map. He shows what the body would look like if each part grew in proportion to the number of sensory neurons it contained. The hands, lips, and mouth are all huge because they are packed with sensory nerves. However, the arms, body, and legs are small and skinny because they have fewer sensory receptors.

WHAT A PAIN

Imagine what would happen if you stepped on a nail or twisted your ankle and it didn't hurt. You could injure yourself more seriously if you didn't know about it right away. That's why your body has special receptors that tell you when something hurts. Your body has more than 3 million pain receptors. Apart from causing a sharp pain to cause you to move away from danger, they also produce a duller pain if you have an injury. The pain stops you from using that part of your body until it heals.

CHANGING YOUR MIND

Human beings are very good at adapting to situations both mentally and physically. You could probably learn to write with your other hand if you broke your arm. Athletes at the Paralympics show the whole world how they can overcome disabilities to take part in their sport. It's all down to finding ways to get the most out of your body, your brain, your senses and your nervous system.

Some blind people can "see" where they're going by making clicking sounds and listening to the echo to judge distances to objects. It's the same method that bats use!

A visually impaired skier has to rely on his sense of hearing to race down the mountain. He listens to his guide and the other sounds he can hear around him.

BRAIN REWIRING

People with poor vision can wear glasses or contact lenses to correct their sight. Hearing aids can help people to hear more clearly. But a person who is completely blind or deaf often uses their other senses to help replace the "missing" sense. Blind people use their sense of touch to read by running their fingertips across raised dots on the surface of Braille pages. Deaf people learn to communicate by lipreading and sign language. Scientists believe that the brain "rewires" itself to use the areas that would otherwise have been devoted to the missing sense.

WHAT ARE YOUR STRENGTHS?

Your brain may be flexible and good at adapting to changing situations, but it still has its strengths and weaknesses. In fact, different areas of your brain do different kinds of work and individual people have varying strengths and skills. You may be excellent with numbers if your frontal lobe is particularly active, or you may prefer arts and languages if your parietal lobe is more developed. You might be great at complicated multiplication problems. Someone else may play the piano brilliantly. Scientists agree that some parts of your brain work better than others.

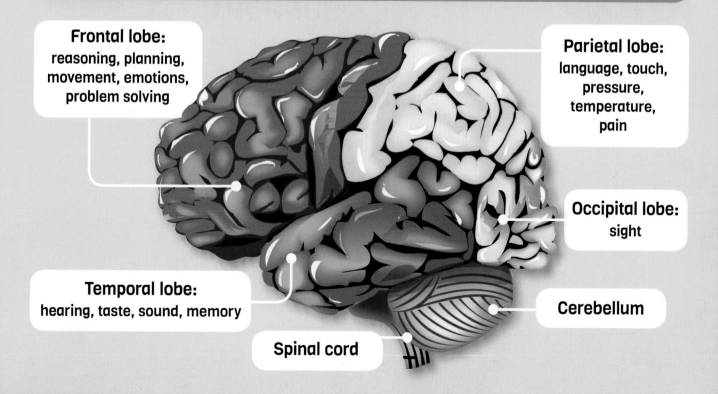

Frontal lobe: reasoning, planning, movement, emotions, problem solving

Parietal lobe: language, touch, pressure, temperature, pain

Occipital lobe: sight

Cerebellum

Temporal lobe: hearing, taste, sound, memory

Spinal cord

BEHIND THE SCENES

Your body has a whole system of automatic-pilot functions that keeps it ticking over. The autonomic nervous system is the central command of this system. Without you being aware of it, this network of nerves controls your breathing, heart rate, swallowing, digestion, blinking, production of saliva, how much you sweat, and whether you need to urinate.

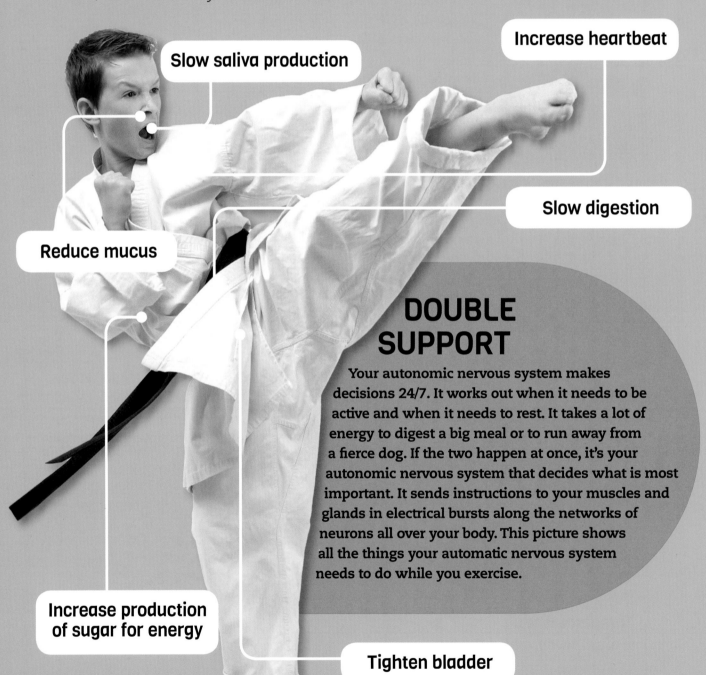

Slow saliva production

Increase heartbeat

Slow digestion

Reduce mucus

Increase production of sugar for energy

Tighten bladder

DOUBLE SUPPORT

Your autonomic nervous system makes decisions 24/7. It works out when it needs to be active and when it needs to rest. It takes a lot of energy to digest a big meal or to run away from a fierce dog. If the two happen at once, it's your autonomic nervous system that decides what is most important. It sends instructions to your muscles and glands in electrical bursts along the networks of neurons all over your body. This picture shows all the things your automatic nervous system needs to do while you exercise.

Your eyes automatically blink around 12 times a minute. So in your lifetime, you will spend about 434 days in darkness due to blinking!

COILED FOR ACTION

The autonomic nervous system springs into action when you're faced with something scary or exciting. It sets up a "fight or flight" response. This gets your heart and lungs to work harder so that you're more alert and have more energy.

REST AND DIGEST

When things are calmer, your digestive system needs oxygen-rich blood to start its job. That's when the autonomic nervous system changes the setting to "rest and digest." Your muscles need less blood, so your heart rate and breathing rate can slow down.

THE BRAIN IN YOUR GUT

A network of about 100 million neurons runs through the lining of your digestive system. It's a special part of the autonomic nervous system, known as the enteric nervous system. Although it has far fewer nerve cells than the brain in your head, scientists sometimes call it your second brain, or the "brain in the gut." It directs the way you digest food and also what to do if it detects something that could make you ill. So if you've ever thrown up after eating something that didn't agree with you, it's time to thank the brain in your gut!

YOUR PERSONAL COMPUTER?

Could a powerful computer do all your thinking just as well as your brain? The computer could certainly do lots of calculating, but it could never take over completely because it can't think or feel for itself. That's where your mind has the advantage. It's all about consciousness.

THINK FOR YOURSELF

Scientists have studied the brain for centuries, but many mysteries remain. They can see how electrical impulses travel from neuron to neuron, and how certain parts of the brain guide your movement, speech, language, and emotions. That much is like looking at a complicated computer, which also has elements to do special jobs. But you're more than a well-run machine. You can choose to do unexpected things, like learning to paraglide, or deciding to take up the saxophone. Could a computer decide to do these things just because it felt like it?

HELPFUL TOOLS

Technology can work alongside the human mind. Advanced computers can even express people's thoughts and feelings. The scientist Stephen Hawking uses a voice simulator to stand in for nerve pathways that have been damaged by disease. But even this advanced technology is obeying orders from the human being who is operating it.

In 1997, world chess champion Garry Kasparov lost to a computer. He then accused the computer of cheating!

CONSCIOUS DECISIONS

Computers can't reproduce what goes on in your mind – that mixture of emotions, feelings and memories that makes you unique. Your mind is aware of all of these. It's responsible for your consciousness, your way of understanding yourself and your place in the world around you. Computers can be programmed to have conversations with people. However, this is just a simulation – a pretend copy of something real. The computer is not aware of itself, and is not thinking like a person would.

FUZZY LOGIC

Computers follow clear instructions to give a correct answer. But they are not very good at thinking imaginatively. If someone asks you what the word "bear" means, you might think of real animals, or a cartoon bear, or a teddy bear you had as a child. A computer couldn't do this.

DID YOU KNOW?

YOUR HEARING ISN'T AS SHARP AFTER YOU HAVE EATEN A BIG MEAL

The chances are that the meal contained food that the body converted into sugar. But a rush of sugar in the bloodstream can affect the way nerves send impulses, especially the sensitive nerves in your ears. So if you're going to a concert, it's best to go easy on the meal beforehand.

PEOPLE CAN SUDDENLY DEVELOP PROFOUND AMNESIA

Amnesia means "memory loss." But unlike many stories in books and films, these people rarely forget who they are. That type of information is part of someone's long-term memory. Instead, people with amnesia usually find it hard to make new memories.

PEOPLE READ UP TO 25 PERCENT FASTER FROM PAPER THAN FROM A COMPUTER SCREEN

That difference seems to be getting smaller as more people grow up reading mainly from screens or tablets. But the theory is that reading from a book helps the reader remember passages more easily because of where they are positioned on the page, on the left, near the top, for example. That's not possible on a screen, and the brain gets a little distracted – and reads more slowly – as a result.

THE CORNEA IN YOUR EYE IS THE ONLY PART OF YOUR BODY WITH NO BLOOD SUPPLY

The cornea must be transparent – so you can see through it – and blood vessels would block your vision. But like other tissue, the cornea needs oxygen to remain healthy. So oxygen in the air dissolves in your tears and spreads throughout the cornea.

EACH DAY YOU THINK ABOUT 70,000 THOUGHTS

This figure is repeated by lots of people – but who originally came up with it, and is it correct? Could the figure even be higher? You're awake for about 50,000 seconds a day, and if you have more than one thought at once ("I'm hungry;" "That car is noisy") each second, then you easily reach 70,000 thoughts, if not more.

SOME PEOPLE CAN HEAR YELLOW OR BLUE

Others might always picture the letter "A" as green, or taste chocolate when they hear a certain song. Scientists believe that some of the neurons and synapses from one sense (smell or hearing, for example) can sometimes cross over to another (such as sight). So a person may end up "smelling" or "hearing" a color.

FREQUENTLY ASKED QUESTIONS

WHY DOES THE DOCTOR TAP YOUR KNEE WITH A HAMMER?

To see how well your nerves carry signals through your body. If they're working well, then your knee will jerk upward. That's because the hammer taps a tendon that connects the muscle to the bone by your knee. The tendon causes the muscle to stretch, sending a nerve impulse to your spinal cord. This impulse triggers another message, which makes the muscle twitch. If the tap doesn't cause a twitch then it might mean you need more tests.

IS IT POSSIBLE TO TICKLE YOURSELF?

No matter how hard you try, you can't manage it. Your brain is constantly dealing with new sensations, sorting out what you see and hear, taste, and touch, to work out whether they are useful or harmful. The ticklish feeling is really a warning – a dangerous spider or insect would tickle you if it crawled up your leg. But your brain considers sensations that you produce yourself as not urgent because it knows you're not facing an unseen threat.

WHY DO PAPER CUTS HURT SO MUCH?

The surface of your skin has more nerve receptors, which send pain signals to your brain, than any other parts of your body. And your fingertips – where you're most likely to get a paper cut – have the most receptors of all. A really serious wound actually destroys some nerve endings, reducing the sense of pain. Paper cuts aren't so serious, which means that the nerve endings survive and continue to send out their signals. Ow!

IS IT YOUR BRAIN HURTING WHEN YOU HAVE A HEADACHE?

Your brain tells you when other parts of your body hurt, but it can't feel pain itself. The bones of your skull and the tissue of your brain don't have the sort of nerves that are sensitive to pain. But the blood vessels that run along the top and base of your brain, and the muscles around your face and jaw, can pass on sensations of pain. The most common headache, a tension headache, is caused when the muscles tighten up in your neck, shoulders, scalp, and jaw.

SYSTEMS OF THE BODY

Skeletal system

The skeletal system supports and protects your body.

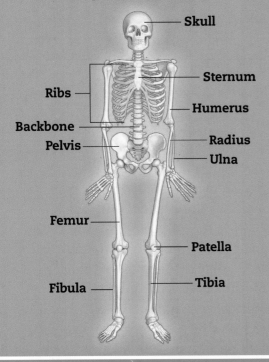

- Skull
- Sternum
- Ribs
- Humerus
- Backbone
- Pelvis
- Radius
- Ulna
- Femur
- Patella
- Fibula
- Tibia

Muscular system

The muscular system moves your body.

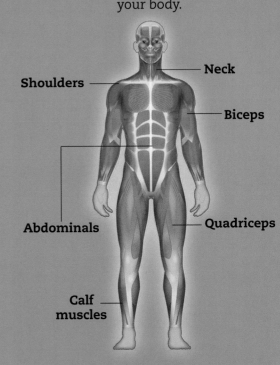

- Neck
- Shoulders
- Biceps
- Abdominals
- Quadriceps
- Calf muscles

Circulatory system

The circulatory system moves blood around your body.

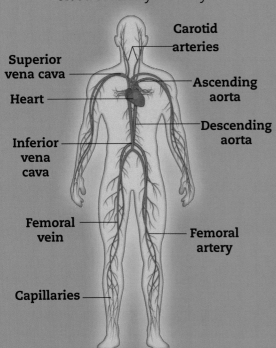

- Carotid arteries
- Superior vena cava
- Ascending aorta
- Heart
- Descending aorta
- Inferior vena cava
- Femoral vein
- Femoral artery
- Capillaries

Respiratory system

The respiratory system controls your breathing.

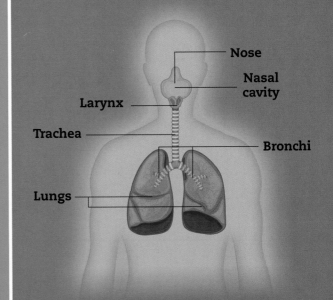

- Nose
- Nasal cavity
- Larynx
- Trachea
- Bronchi
- Lungs

This is your quick reference guide to the main systems of the body: skeletal, muscular, respiratory, circulatory, digestive, nervous, endocrine, and lymphatic.

Digestive system

The digestive system takes food in and out of your body.

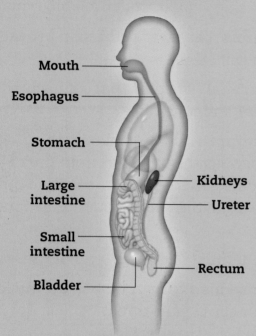

Mouth
Esophagus
Stomach
Large intestine
Kidneys
Ureter
Small intestine
Rectum
Bladder

Nervous system

The nervous system carries messages around your body and controls everything you do.

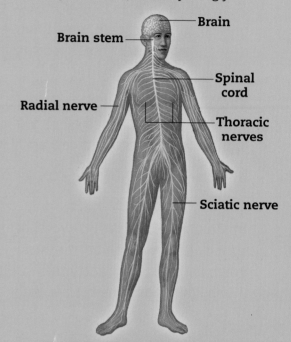

Brain
Brain stem
Spinal cord
Radial nerve
Thoracic nerves
Sciatic nerve

Endocrine system

The endocrine system produces hormones and controls your growth and mood.

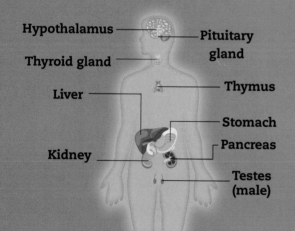

Hypothalamus
Pituitary gland
Thyroid gland
Thymus
Liver
Stomach
Pancreas
Kidney
Testes (male)

Ovaries (female)

Lymphatic system

The lymphatic system fights off germs and helps keep your body healthy.

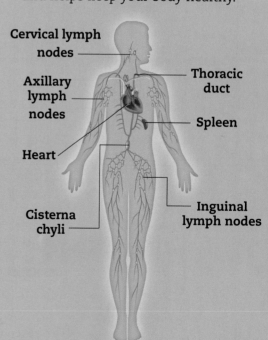

Cervical lymph nodes
Thoracic duct
Axillary lymph nodes
Spleen
Heart
Cisterna chyli
Inguinal lymph nodes

GLOSSARY

autonomic nervous system The network of nerves that controls your breathing, heart rate, swallowing, digestion, blinking, and production of saliva, sweat, and urine.

axon The long, slender part of a nerve cell that passes electrical signals away from the cell body.

bladder The organ that stores urine in the body.

brain stem The part of your brain that connects with your spinal cord. It looks after activities such as digestion, blood flow, and breathing.

cerebellum The area at the back of your brain that controls all your movements.

cerebrum The part of the brain that includes the frontal, parietal, temporal, and occipital lobes.

cochlea The spiral-shaped structure in the inner ear.

cornea The transparent front part of the eye.

dendrite The part of a nerve cell that picks up signals from other neurons.

dermis The layer of the skin beneath the epidermis.

ear canal The tube that connects the outer and inner ear.

eardrum A thin membrane that separates the outer ear from the middle ear. It transmits sounds from the air to the small bones of the inner ear.

epidermis The outer layer of the skin.

Eustachian tube A tube that connects your ear to your throat.

frequency (of a sound wave) The speed at which a sound wave vibrates, which determines its pitch.

frontal lobe The area of the brain that deals with reasoning, movement, emotions, and problem-solving.

hormone A chemical that helps to regulate processes such as reproduction and growth.

immune system The network of organs, chemicals, and special cells that protects the body from disease.

iris The colored part of the eye that opens and closes to control the amount of light entering the eye.

motor neuron One of the nerve cells that carry messages from the brain and the muscles.

mucus A slippery substance produced by the body to protect against infection.

neuron (nerve cell) One of the basic cells of the nervous system.

occipital lobe The area of the brain that deals with sight.

optic nerve The nerve that links the eyes and the brain.

parietal lobe The area of the brain that deals with language, touch, pressure, temperature, and pain.

pinna The visible part of the outer ear.

pupil (in the eye) The hole in the center of the iris that allows light to enter the eye.

retina The area at the back of the eye that contains millions of receptor cells.

saliva The liquid in your mouth that begins the process of digestion.

sensory neuron One of the nerve cells that carry messages from the senses to the brain.

spinal cord A collection of nerves that runs from your brain down the middle of the back and ends at your waist. Nerves branch out from it to run to the rest of your body.

synapse The small gap that separates neurons.

temporal lobe The area of the brain that deals with hearing, taste, sound and memory.

thoracic nerve One of the twelve nerves that emerge from the spinal cord in the upper body.

FURTHER READING

Body Works by Anna Claybourne (QED Publishing, 2014)

Complete Book of the Human Body by Anna Claybourne (Usborne Books, 2013)

Everything You Need to Know about the Human Body by Patricia MacNair (Kingfisher, 2011)

Horrible Science: Body Owner's Handbook by Nick Arnold (Scholastic Press, 2014)

Mind Webs: Human Body by Anna Claybourne (Wayland, 2014)

Project Science: Human Body by Sally Hewitt (Franklin Watts, 2012)

INDEX